D1623008

All the Best from Bikini Bottom

by David Lewman

SCHOLASTIC INC.

New York Toronto London Auckland Sydney
Mexico City New Delhi Hong Kong Buenos Aires

Based on the TV series *SpongeBob SquarePants*® created by
Stephen Hillenburg as seen on Nickelodeon®

ISBN 0-439-72400-7

12 11 10 9 8 7 6 5 4 3 2 1   5 6 7 8 9 10/0

Printed in the U.S.A.   08

First Scholastic printing, March 2005

You always paid close attention in class.

Sure,
maybe you got behind once or twice,
BUT YOU DID IT!

**Great job, pardner!
Graduatin' can be tougher than
wrestlin' a giant clam!**

Yay, graduation!

Goooooooooooo,

GRADUATE!

Big deal. I went to college.

TIPS FOR THE BIG DAY

First things first:
You'll want to be very clean for graduation.

You'll
want to
get
dressed
up.

And please go to the bathroom
before
the ceremony.

- Don't panic—plenty of graduates have ripped their pants.

- If you're wearing a graduation robe, relax! The robe'll cover the rip. (Unless you rip the robe, too.)

- If you're not wearing a graduation robe, try to get all the other grads to rip their pants so you'll match.

- Use a marker to quickly color your underpants the same color as your pants.

- Use the tassel on your graduation cap to sew up the rip.

- Say "Look, everyone, it's Mermaidman!" While they're looking, borrow Patrick's shorts.

- If all else fails, just show your ripped pants to everybody. At least you'll get a big laugh!

Greetings, members of the Mermaidman fan club. I mean graduates.

Congratulations on graduating from this school, no matter how hard the Dirty Bubble tried to stop you.

So, in conclusion, if you want to grow up big and strong like me, remember to eat your milk and drink your vegetables. And always be on the lookout for . . .

EEEEEVIIIIIIITTUUUUUUU!

I'm supposed to give a speech to my fellow graduates at the Bikini Bottom Academy of Modern Dance and Clarinet Playing. But some of the words are missing. Will you help me by filling in the blanks?

(An adjective is a word that describes things, like *rotten* or *smelly*. A noun is a thing, like *pizza*. A verb is an action word, like *eat* or *burp*. An adverb is a word that describes a way of doing something, like *slowly* or *happily*.)

Dear Fellow Graduates of _____,
school name

When I look out on your _____ faces,
adjective

I am filled with _____. We've worked
kind of food

really _____, but we've also had a lot
adverb

of _____.
noun

Of course we couldn't have done it without

_____. Thanks to _____, we
teacher name   teacher name

learned how to _____, _____,
verb   verb

and even _____. I really loved the
verb

_____ing!
verb

So remember, keep your _____s on
body part

the _____, and your _____ on
noun   body part

the _____!
noun

Thank you, and good _____!
noun

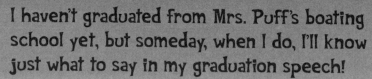

I haven't graduated from Mrs. Puff's boating school yet, but someday, when I do, I'll know just what to say in my graduation speech!

Fellow boating-school graduates, we've been through a lot together—a lot of boating. We've boated forward, and we've boated backward. We've boated to the right, and we've boated to the left, which I still have trouble with.

But thanks to the greatest boating teacher in the world, Mrs. Puff, we've learned how to boat with the best of boaters . . . boatily.

So let me just say in conclusion that
I'M READY . . . TO DRIVE A BOAT!

Come on, fellow boaters, let's get out there and boat!

Thank you.

STUFF GRADUATES KNOW

1. One Krabby Patty plus one Krabby Patty equals delicious

2. How to spell weird words like "dry" and "land"

3. The complete history of Bikini Bottom

4. Who all the kings of the sea were (so far, just Neptune)

5. The science of blowing bubbles

6. The life cycle of the jellyfish

7. How to draw a starfish

8. How to draw a starfish into a restaurant (of course, *everyone* knows that!)

THE BEST PART OF GRADUATING:
THE CELEBRATION!

You'll figure out the best way to celebrate your graduation, because you're a deep thinker.

And as we say at the Krusty Krab, every party needs a patty.

And if a party's not quite your
speed, you could
ride sea horses . . .

or catch up on your sleep.

zzzzz

You could relax and take it easy . . .

or go on a road trip with your best friend.

One of the best things about graduating is all the gifts you'll receive. As a responsible graduate, your first undertaking is to tackle the thank-you notes. We've made it easy for you. Just fill in the blanks!

Dear _____,
_____name of gift-giver_____

Thank you so much for the _____
_____adjective_____

_____. It sure is _____.
_____noun_____   _____adjective_____

I love to go _____ing, so it'll
_____verb_____

come in real handy every time I go to the

_____.
_____location_____

I'll treasure your gift for _____,
_____a period time_____

Love,

_____
_____your name_____

P.S. Today I'm using your gift as a(n)

_____ to _____ my
_____noun_____   _____verb_____

_____. It works like a(n)
_____noun_____

_____!
_____noun_____

With so many possibilities and choices to make, you may feel like you are having a hard time standing on two feet.

But just remember that life after graduation is full of surprises—you never know what you might find!

Who knows what heights you'll reach?

a doctor...

or maybe a lawyer.

Maybe you'll own a business and make boatloads of money!

Or if you're really lucky, you'll land the greatest job of all—working at the Krusty Krab!

GRADUATE, I SALUTE YOU.

Go have some fun. And remember,
no matter what you decide to do next . . .

you're sure to be a
star.